spirit unyielding

# spirit unyielding

sarie hwang

illustrated with love by dear glor

Copyright © 2023 Sarie Hwang

All rights reserved. No part of this publication may be reproduced, distributed or transmitted in any form or by any means, including photocopying, recording, or other electronic or mechanical methods, without the prior written permission of the publisher, except in the case of brief quotations embodied in critical reviews and certain other noncommercial uses permitted by copyright law.

ISBN: 979-8-218-33813-8

for those who persist in hope, yearning to believe in the light awaiting them at the tunnel's end.

*my beloved speaks and says to me:*
*'arise, my love, my beautiful one, and come away,*
*for behold, the winter is past; the rain is over and gone'.*

— solomon

lost in shadows, a journey to reclaim light

## *contents*

| | |
|---|---:|
| here, but my soul is weary | 1 |
| yet i persevere | 21 |
| at tunnel's end | 45 |
| the path, ever unwinding | 65 |
| epilogue: traces of the soul | 95 |

## *here, but my soul is weary*

a raw glimpse into the intricate inner workings of the human psyche, exploring emptiness, guilt, longing, and the ever-present question of who we truly are.

***hypnotic glow***

endless nights,
sleep a stranger to my eyes.
but i resist its tempting embrace,
tomorrow's fatigue can bear the weight.
i succumb to the hypnotic scroll,
work looms ahead—
what am i doing?
its emptiness consumes me,
a zombie ensnared by the screen's glow,
lost in the grip of the night.
it's okay, no one knows,
and so it goes,
and then i repeat this ritual,
tomorrow night.

### *empty vessel*

for a long time,
my cup remained empty.
then arrived company,
infusing my solitude with joy.
it kept my cup full for a span,
yet, in time, it ceased to satisfy.
i sought other avenues,
to fill this void within my cup.
i found, none could quench its depths.
left parched and desolate,
i conceded,
proceeded with an empty vessel,
its offerings now exhausted.

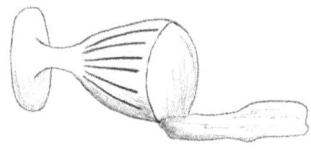

## *a fracture*

too much,
or not enough?
lost in between,
i pursued balance,
though it remained elusive.
motivated to be average
for the past decade,
yet an unfamiliar face
gazes from the glass.
*who am i*, really?
i concealed my essence
to fit their mold,
my authentic being
they deemed excessive.

### *my intentions*

i wanted to ask—how are you doing?
but my words became a knot in my throat.
i don't think i have the heart to ask,
knowing that things aren't well.
guilt clings to me like a stubborn stain,
and for years i've been struggling to say:

i know you're doing your best,
i'm sorry i haven't been by your side.
i wish i could do more,
but i don't seem to know how.
is there anything i can do for you?
no really, you deserve the world.
but i'm afraid she won't believe these words,
rightfully so—i haven't been there for her,
cowardice led to only a few guilt-ridden texts.
i'm so sorry, i really am.

## *veiled delight*

brightest as ever—recounting my tale of woe,
their faces perplexed, uncertain where to go.
to laugh, offer comfort, or dismiss my strain?
i feel their emotions, they judge me insane.

it's not an amusing tale, i agree,
yet my words stumble as i strive to tell my story,
my silent plea, someone help me cope,
please catch on, i can only hope.

layers beneath, unknown by all,
i part with a smile, it's my disappointing call.

### *deceit is a heavy burden*

the speck in your eyes
still lingers in my thoughts.
if only you'd change,
i'd find some peace of mind.

i plan to tell you:
there's a significant flaw,
that it's amiss,
bearing a hurtful sting,
if it's not thoughtlessness—
perhaps it will be deemed two-faced.
please, take care of it.

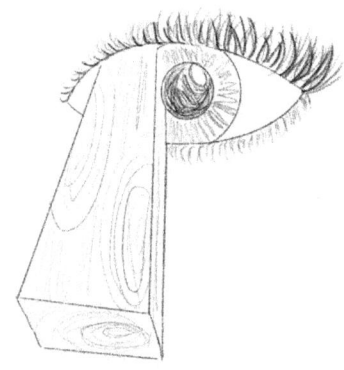

i left unsaid:
i'm sharing, at my own expense,
suffering the burden of confrontation,
the mark of a loyal friend.
i pray, you realize,
it's genuinely for your own sake.

yet, why this sense of deceit—
with every fiber of my being?
the weight of hypocrisy,
a heavy load to carry.
the plank in my own eye,
it's there, i'm aware.
why have i become this?
i hate it all,
but myself, most of all.

## *this emotion is "hurt"*

beginning marked by innocence,
i loved, depths untold,
cherished our bond,
my soul, freely poured out,
pursuing a profound connection,
craving meaning and worth.
my heart i gave,
so naively,
believing in forever,
oblivious to the gap.

as time flowed,
frustration sprouted,
disappointment found a place,
resentment placed in my heart,
words unspoken and feelings sore,
inarticulate, in that unfamiliar terrain.
a season marked by a baffling display,
realized, the emotion was hurt,
a wounded heart from one you love,
priceless lessons learned.

i won't love,
at my own expense,
though they remain unaware,
the heartache persists.
innocence, now a memory dear,
sadly, i've changed.

## *daily recurrences*

i justify
silently—
rationale for
my choices
that underwhelm;
deception's refuge
transiently,
until old troubles
bubble yet again.

## *essence of it all*

they said, stop
i asked, why
their retort, ugh
i countered, ha
they boiled, mad
i withered, sad
they revealed, foe
i shrank, hurt
they urged, chill
i waived, bye

## *daily soliloquy*

"i hate you."
the refrain that echoed most—
was in my own voice,
aimlessly unleashed.
i'm sorry,
if these words were spoken to you,
they weren't;
i wasn't sure of their origin,
or their target.
i'm not loathsome,
i don't harbor hate in my heart,
at least not for you.
when i faced a mirror,
the reflection stared back;
then i *grasped*,
these aimless words,
were spoken to myself.

## *feign*

i yield,
concluded, this is it,
it's passable, yet sufficient,
happiness at its extent—
for *me*.
rest assured,
this genuinely appeals,
contentment resides within my heart,
in this diluted rendition
of what could be.
a surface merely scratched,
all glitter, no gold.
an illusion of dreams achieved,
it keeps me in pretense.

## *projection*

you asked,
"are you doing alright?"

in defense, i resisted,
"are *you*?"

your response,
"sorry, i was concerned."

i lashed out, creating distance,
sensing vulnerability drawing near,
then, i shuddered—
what if everyone knows?
what a daunting thought,
detaching once more,
i'll deal with it another day.

### *we used to be close*

i remember,
when we used to be close—
sharing hearts,
enjoying company
of a kindred soul...
blissfully ignorant.
even the best of times,
are not everlasting.

 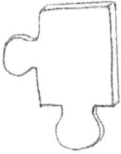

## *existential crisis*

what i cherished—
it dawned on me,
is meaningless.
pretense of
pleasure,
fulfillment,
and
assurance,
in my nature:
ever-changing,
fickle,
feelings unreliable.

## *unsaid goodbyes*

i thanked you, though barely audible,
my next words refused to surface.
if i had spoken more, tears would have flowed,
choking on my throat, swallowed my heartache.

i really appreciate your thoughtfulness,
your care and kindness, they don't go unnoticed.
i'm sorry i'm sensitive, both my flaw and strength.
i truly love and value you, though words seem to
    escape me.

honestly, i don't think you understand—
just how much you mean to me.
i won't blame you if you feel i'm ungrateful,
but please, don't be sad; my love for you runs deep.

praying the unspoken words find their way,
justified to myself—i'm not entitled; i'm struggling to
    convey.
we said goodbye, uncertain of our next encounter,
but know that you hold a cherished place beyond
    words...

## *duality of being*

say one thing, think another
desire goodness, perform evil
sometimes sweet, sometimes sour
preach gratitude, seldom felt
masked warmth, lingering frost
smile outside, tears well up
apathetic, affections concealed
intrigued, feign indifference
speak harshly, i know you love deeply
heartbroken, yet unbroken
hope persists, spirit unyielding

*yet i persevere*

a look into the enduring spirit that lies within, embracing hope and tenacity, and re-learning the self, while acknowledging the invaluable support of those who stand by us.

## *disenchanted*

i pray,
the same words,
like a broken record's song,
yet, change remains elusive,
once more and again,
sowing disillusionment within my heart,
apathy cradling.
it's exhausting to care so deeply,
only to be met by sadness...
can you feel my heartache?
it's fine,
i don't presume you can.

## *whispers during the tempest*

treasured jewel,
in its purest form.
why then,
do you perceive
a replaceable stone?
you are not—
a fleeting indulgence.
you are God's royalty,
precious and cherished.

*promise*

to that place,
i journey daily,
heart full of anticipation,
yearning for our encounter.

yet, i'm here today,
hope-fueled steps let down—
*where are You?*
silence echoes in response.

still, i reassure my soul,
it's alright,
tomorrow holds promise anew.

## *my dearly loved*

i miss the sound of your voice on the phone,
the taste of your cooking, it was my favorite thing.
i cherish our memory of going to the countryside, to
    your home;
it was just me and you, on the train.
immaturity had me complaining, now i see,
you gifted me these mementos, precious recollections...
and all my life—i relished in the warmth of your love
    for me.
this world feels a little emptier without you,
how i wish you were still here.

## *meaning*

the mundane, a silent muse,
shapes me in its unadorned way,
crafting character and nurturing bonds.

not everything demands meaning, you see,
nor proves it prudent in our every pursuit.
substance resides in embracing life's ebb and flow.

in moments like these,
significance finds its voice through:
the fragrant bloom of kindness,
the unyielding roots of endurance,
and the nurturing sunlight of responsibility's tender
    grace.

## *a glimpse of it*

are they still near?
i think they departed.
it's alright, i understand,
i'm alone again.

wait, they're still here?
why would they linger?
perhaps they empathize,
maybe they truly care.

some stay for a lifetime,
true friends never stray.
their presence brings comfort,
and strength to persevere.

### *my heart holds you, everyday*

apple of my eye,
kin unlike any other,
nostalgia calls.

you have no idea,
how i pray for you daily,
hoping for your joy.

*courage*

in the storm of loneliness,
a little courage stretches far,
look around, caring souls surround,
embrace their hand, don't shy away.

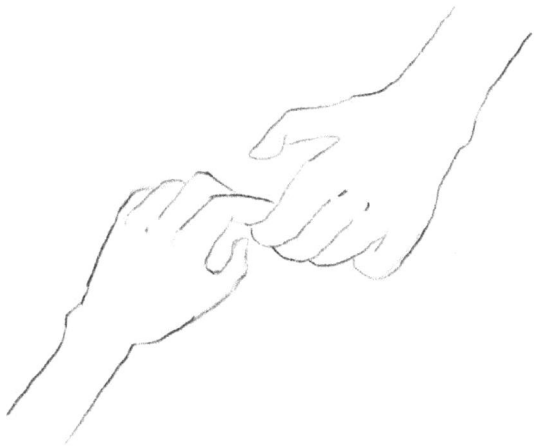

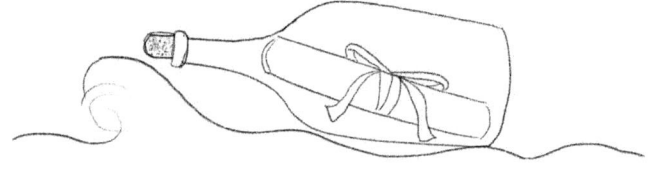

*sometimes i wonder*

sometimes i wonder
if my words will ever reach you,
that you might understand,
my true intention and heart.

### *kindred soul*

a rare encounter,
an unforeseen connection,
you're a gift from God.

*introspection*

often undervalued is a rich inner world:
one that delves beneath the surface,
ponders the meaning of existence,
meditates on Creator's intentions,
treasures introspection's bittersweet embrace,
contemplates unconventional notions.
a priceless rarity,
embraced by those who hunger.

### *them*

they don't see me,
talk *as if* they understand.
judgments are made
based on my shell.

as for me,
i tell myself:
they'll come to see
if we're meant to be.

*you*

yet you, my dear,
you *see* me.
you don't care
what they say.

i can feel it,
your kind soul,
you look out for me.
we're meant to be.

## *following the heart*

the path of the heart seems effortless,
yet choices ripple outward, affecting all.
you, dear, bear the deepest scars,
from choices complacent;
caution being lured astray by feelings deceiving,
the kind that is transient and fleeting,
anchoring you in place for far too long.
early endeavors may feel like daunting waves,
truth is, lasting implications run far deeper,
and courage, at times, sets us apart—
it may mean veering from the heart's desire,
to take the road less traveled,
for your sake, and yours alone.

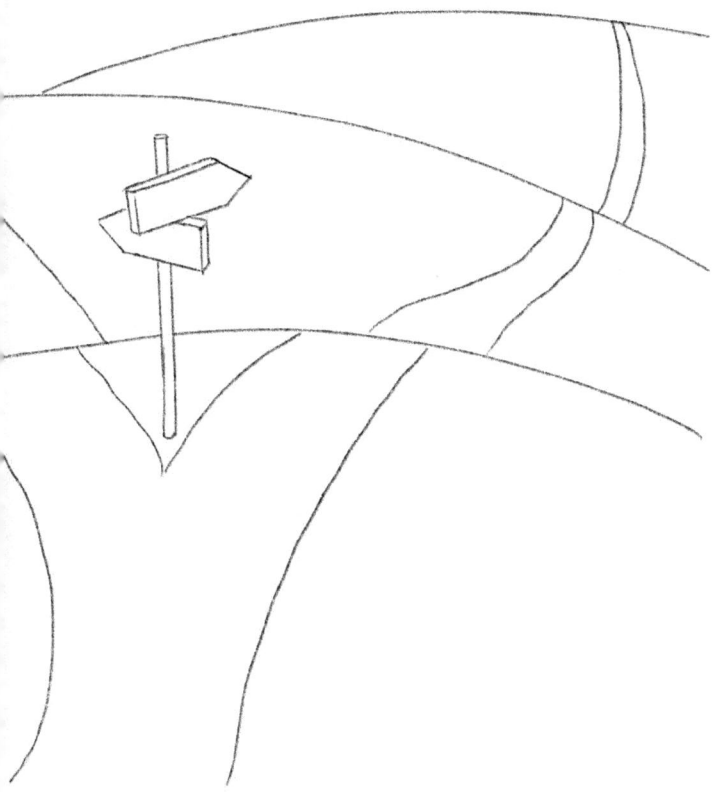

## *legacy of worth*

what truly merits our time on earth—
riches and renown, or love and family?
what brings lasting joy,
satiating ceaseless longings?
what's worth dwelling on,
what legacy will we leave behind?

daunted by commitment, in denial of it all,
inadequacy and fears loom,
i need faith, courage to see it through.
then, tranquility settles in knowing,
You're the source of my strength.

## *faith*

i'm determined to believe,
that intention resides,
in every being.
a purpose for life,
i'm curious about mine,
it will unravel in time.

## *journey*

same thing, every day,
striving for the unseen, come what may.
no harvest yet; it's okay—
valued things need time.

i persist, dedicating my hours
to forgotten pursuits, now realigned,
long-sought dreams are finally mine.
this journey is precious, in the process,
and worthwhile, because You've been by my side.

results unfold precisely, at the intended time,
so i press on, ever forward.

## *intentionally designed*

because,
you—
are special.
crafted uniquely;
*you* are meant to be.
you are you—
by intentional design,
not by happenstance.
a precious soul,
none can replace;
deeply treasured,
you are beloved.

## *at tunnel's end*

the resilient passage from darkness to light, witnessing restoration, experiencing the transformative power of love, and culminating in the hopeful realization of light at the end of the tunnel.

## *the tides will turn*

valleys come, in the dead of night,
without warning, no hint in sight.
mountains rise, in the changing season,
imperceptibly, without rhyme or reason.

### *you make me hope*

how—
do you trust me,
as i grapple with doubts within my core?
what do you discern within me,
that eludes my own perception?
what makes you say
that i'm deserving of admiration
when my reflection in the glass
fails to show my worth?

my progress thus far,
i owe to your words,
you glimpsed my potential,
underneath the veil.
this poem is for you,
for hope was sown by your trust.

## *unfolding*

my thoughts are fluid,
ever-changing,
don't stay put,
but why should they?

i'm evolving,
learning at each step,
paradigm shifts,
essential turning points.

## *what is love?*

at first, i fell in love...
sparks gone, quickly faded,
bored of lukewarm embrace,
yet friendship kept us close.
years passed—
i hit lows, you remained,
showing love,
unconditionally,
caring without reservation.
my heart touched,
again, and again,
my love grew.
an understanding of love,
because of your love,
i love you.

## *my aspiration*

i learn from you, for you bear light,
your kindness and humility, a glowing sight.
without need to project, to boast or berate,
your pure intentions, they resonate and radiate.

it offers hope, inspires a humble heart,
a gentle nudge to calm, before i fall apart.
to analyze the gains, i contemplate,
"what's in it for me?" i'd calculate.

so i thank you, dear one, for all you do,
i aspire to be that person, because of you.

## *you're a work of art*

my deluded notion of progress,
going against my grain,
brought relief but left a mess,
a cost paid by my future in pain.

dear reader, listen thus:
you're a work of art, not an anomaly,
crafted with a purpose beyond mere bliss,
not to conform to mediocrity.

*surrender*

i relinquish,
of treasures i once held high and true,
they've become an empty echo,
amidst it all, remains only You.

### *light approaches*

tomorrow, my hero,
in the midst of today's distress,
the light approaches,
agony's end, in slow progress.

this is a moment to savor,
an intimate memory in the making,
"i miss it there," i'll fondly recall.
times of growth, of perseverance,
when courage won over pain's reign,
and faith kept me ever enduring.

inspired by the journey, not of my making,
though struggles persist,
until that awaited day's embrace,
stay steadfast on the course,
for the end is nearing.

forget it's on the horizon,
and soon you'll find you've arrived.

## *resilience*

i was struggling.
people, i thought, laughed,
at me—
inadequate and inept.
disappointed,
by expectations unmet.
the urge to flee,
to hide from everything.
instead, i stayed,
sobbing beneath my covers,
enduring long and demanding days.
the clouds began to part,
though it took time,
its duration, underestimated.
progress revealed itself,
when least expected.

### *when you check in on me, again*

you returned and asked,
"are you alright?"

desperate, i cried,
"help me, please."

vulnerability took hold,
honesty poured forth,
fearing their response,
i closed my eyes, tears rolling down,
imagined judgment, insecurity blooming.

but, to my surprise, your words were kind,
"i'm here for you, how can i support?"

taken aback, i murmured,
"nothing, just stay by my side."

with a smile, you reassured,
"i care for you, i'll do my best."

humbled, i realized,
i'd been harsh on us both.

## *heart's nudge*

voice inside whispered:
"you're a burden,
to those nearby.
they give love,
you bring despair."

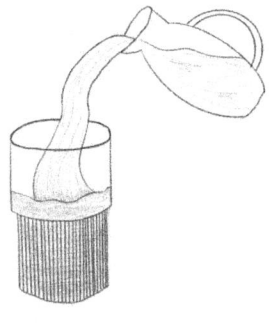

for what do i live
if i only hurt?
a wounded soul,
i persuaded myself,
my existence,
only steals joy away.

yet, my heart nudged—
it took a little courage,
to take the first step.
one step led to another,
then i saw it unfold...
my cup being filled.

at last, love to share.

## *heart brimming with...*

my heart, once full
of unforgiveness,
where bitterness entrenched,
each hurt cherished, a burdened chest.

i confess,
dwelling granted comfort,
though but a deceptive veneer...
emotions laid dormant,
true depth eluded my embrace.
a heart stagnated by contrived injustice,
so full, yet too numb to feel,
apathetic, yet craving affection,
yearning, yet calloused.

in the presence of God, humbled,
a prayer whispered, surrendering,
desiring selfless love, generosity.

acknowledging,
i've been hurt in the past,
but clinging proved futile.

my longing,
to cradle love, not its semblance;
no cheap substitutes will suffice.
for nothing else carries weight,
meaning dissolves in its luminous presence.

now i know,
to receive, i had to empty—
season squandered grasping at shadows,
gratitude blossoms in hindsight,
all those heartaches, products of selfishness.

my heart now full
of gratitude and humility,
an intentional choice, pursuing joy.

### *unexpected guest*

joy returned,
uninvited.
a beautiful twist,
when least expected.
embrace the sunrise with glee,
slumber's solace, freed,
blissfully envisioning,
when my labor bears fruit,
and my dreams do come true.

***pinch me, because this reality is too good to be real***

the sweetest haven,
a gentle, loving embrace.
peace in knowing,
everything will be okay.
not mere wishful thinking,
nor denial of reality—
a faith that's lived and felt.

## *a feast awaits*

a tender whisper calls me near,
hesitant, i wander, with curiosity my guide,
a world so vast, where marvels do appear,
i shrug, the world is my oyster here.

not long after, the luster wanes,
this, i sense, cannot satisfy.
mustering courage, i conclude,
let's retrace, reassess.

with cautious steps, i pass the familiar door,
and there, i *gasp*, my breath stolen away...

it's been set all along—
a feast awaits, Father's table.

### *restoration*

darkness surrounds me, where is the light?
hope has fled, leaving me to fight.
help, does anyone hear my plea?
please, someone save me.

i've journeyed far, lost sight of the light,
start walking, even if odds feel slight.
beyond reach, is it a false affair?
impossible, i've seen it there.

"you're doing great," i hear.
this inexplicable faith, i hold dear.
is that the light? i sense it near.
at tunnel's end, a brightness so clear.

in the light, thank you Jesus.

## *the path, ever unwinding*

what lies beyond the tunnel? emotions weave a tapestry—steadfast in the pursuit of purpose, embracing dear ones, and reflecting on the remarkable resilience of the human spirit to find its way back to the light.

## *homebound*

traveler by day,
dreamer by night,
carried by wanderlust,
unburdened by the mundane.

i'm happy-go-lucky,
others fear tomorrow.
yet, i dream of the day,
in the haven of home,
where my spirit finds rest.

roaming is purposeful,
yet home is forever.
when that day finds me,
i'll reminisce with fondness,
bearing no sorrow,
in the moments gone by.

## *like an onion*

*first layer shed*
"i'm enlightened," i said,
then, puzzling gaps emerged.

*second layer shed*
"this feels genuinely profound," i nodded,
yet new complexities unfurled.

*third layer shed*
"finally, this rings truer than the rest," i rejoiced,
only to find myself in an unfamiliar landscape.

*fourth layer shed*
failing to grasp the wisdom,
i proudly expressed, "i'm in harmony with myself,"
but soon, the tides swiftly turned.

*fifth layer shed*
skeptical, i cautiously remarked, "we'll see,"
and once more, tensions heightened.

*sixth layer shed*
i perceive the recurring design,
the mystery of infinite revelation,
even within my own soul.
that's the wonder;
"a lifetime's exploration," i acknowledged.

*seventh layer shed*
humbled, i whispered,
"countless layers remain, i'm certain,"
yet each season unfolds with its unique gift.

## *what could be*

what if,
in this alternate rendition of existence,
the world unfurls like an endless oyster,
and you're *free* to dream—
imagination unleashed,
you're frolicking like a child,
strength flowing from the eternal fount of life,
an infinite reservoir.
you partake in what you require,
your bill is settled,
lying in the fullness of existence,
living the life meant for you.

## *soulmate*

do soulmates exist? i wondered,
i'm not too sure about you, i mused,
a sea of differences, i suggested,
no ember of passion, i admitted,
we're on different wavelengths, i concluded.

yet, what is the essence of a soulmate?
my eyes sparkled with curiosity.

affection transcending mere attraction,
partnership surpassing the realms of friendship,
togetherness through divergence's tides,
interdependent, each with its distinct melody,
amidst it all, finding unmatched solace.

being with you, i'm me, yet elevated.
and i've reached the conclusion—
soulmates do exist.

## *words that stayed with me*

nonchalantly, he shared,
"i love my home."

curious, i probed,
"don't you feel alive when you're out in the world?"

without blinking, he expressed,
"no, i enjoy being home."

teasingly, i persisted,
"what if we moved to a new state?"

with certainty, he replied,
"home is anywhere with you."

### *the only constant is change*

in life's loftiest summits and its deepest abyss,
with cherished souls or an opulent feast's bliss,
in the comfort of the mundane or the excitement of
    the new,
through jobless winters or the anchor of employment,
perhaps in your mood today or in tomorrow's fears,
remember, this too shall pass,
and everything will be okay, in time, my dear.

### *how are you?*

i miss you, too,
how do you do?
i have no clue,
if you're feeling it too.

so i'll just assume,
our hearts are in tune,
souls of a kind,
hard to unwind.

"are you happy?" i ask,
"i'm happy too," to bask,
but i think my soul,
misses your soul.

reality may divide,
your essence resides,
dwelling in my heart,
now worlds apart.

## *we used to be close, part two*

i sometimes miss it...
but we've outgrown each other,
we each have companions,
who now inhabit that space.
some people only stay
for a momentary coexistence,
but the mementos of our time,
reside in my heart.

### *relinquish what no longer serves*

i'll admit it now:
she was smarter and more precise, her voice resonating
 louder.
at the time, i couldn't fully grasp—
we were both enduring, two hurting souls;
no harm was intended at me, specifically.
but, feeling victimized, i convinced myself,
"we're nothing more than strangers, if not enemies."

as time unfolded, amidst our shared growth,
i reached an understanding: each of us doing the best
 we know.
gratitude for her fills me, and i pray,
for her happiness and ever-expanding journey.
love gently burns in my heart.

***transience***

joy is fleeting,
a passing breeze—
a mindful act
to cherish it,
to remember it,
to extend it,
in gratitude,
share its warmth,
in its transience,
and it returns,
before i know it.

## *i still pray for you*

you're a memory box i gently unlock,
to savor the sweetness of the past we've woven,
shared nostalgia, a tapestry unbroken,
smiling one moment, then i'm in tears.

yet, it's a well i dare not frequent,
emotions, like waves, leave me spent,
i ache for the past, for you, my dear,
but you're distant, and i'm filled with regret.

if these verses find you, please know,
i still pray for you—
your joy is my only intention,
in a world where you feel loved and cherished.

until that day arrives, i'll continue praying,
and open up our memory box, from time to time,
our stories unbroken and my spirit unburdened.

## *unaddressed letter*

my darling,

do you miss me like i miss you?
do you feel my absence sometimes?
do old photos make you reminisce?
or have you moved on...
found my replacement?
no one can truly fill your presence,
i fear they don't exist.
but take your time; your place remains.
my heart still carries you—
and i love you more than you know.

ever adoring,
your dearest

## *my forte*

"too sensitive,"

i was told, that ever-so-familiar tune,
once it pierced, my identity fractured,
placed doubt in what i felt.

through wiser eyes, i've come to find,
it's my unique grace, there's no shame.
no longer a burden, i happily say:

"thanks for the compliment;
it's my superpower, come what may."

## *amends*

i couldn't be happy for you then,
complex emotions, hard to express,
regrets, you need not comprehend,
i created that, nothing less.

i want to be the happiest—
*for you*, in every single win.
i'm here, the truest,
with you through thick and thin.

## *old friend*

an old friend
returned, unannounced,
whispered in my ears,
why i'm worthless,
how i'm undeserving,
of love, of kinship.

i curled up in bed,
drowned in self-pity
until the veil lifted—
it never was my friend,
an unwelcome company.
our trajectories
no longer intertwine.

farewell,
ghost of the past,
our journey ends here.

## *good news*

in moments of such boundless joy,
yearning to share this sacred space,
of love, of triumph, kindred hearts aligned,
stirred fervently, unconfined.

it longs to be expressed,
brightly named, glorified,
with those around, hearts interlacing,
a telepathy, emotions embracing.

it's that same feeling,
the one i want to proclaim.
that it's really true—
i am loved by God.

## *it may not seem that way, but it'll be okay*

the first time, i despaired,
fearful—
reality had inverted its tale,
yes, i'm the architect of my failure,
yet, in reflection, i discovered,
seasons ebbed and flowed.
and, above all else,
there was hope.

the second time, i carried shame,
internalized my pain,
pointed fingers inward, once more.
still, i clung, unwavering,
for deep within, i believed,
hope persisted.
in hindsight, i unearthed,
change is often a friend,
bringing more joy than sorrow—
i reaped beyond my humblest hopes.

the third time, i embraced.
truly, i didn't die,
it's not the world's final curtain.
for all things unfold with reason,
and seasons do come and go—
surrender to the present's grace.
my heart, flows with peace,
and i thank you, dear Jesus,
i feel Your tender care for my individual life.

## *my asset*

beloved souls, the ones i love,
my treasures, the very riches of my heart.
as the sun descends beneath the horizon's line,
what stirs the spirit is the profound essence of love.
for what holds greater worth,
than a human soul, our most precious joy?
when our stories are told, what wealth compares?

## *always, smiling*

you make me smile,
both good days and bad,
a fateful intersection,
i thank God above.

imperfect souls,
forever evolving,
we're in it together,
hearts intertwining.

### *quality time*

soul-searching days,
pondering my purpose in this life.
sunlight's gentle grace caresses my face,
in tranquil serenity, i pray:

Lord,
how will you use me?
will there come a moment i say,
"for this, i was created?"

lost in joyful tears,
i drift into a dreamy reverie,
a life transcending the self,
beyond mere happiness and comfort.
there must be more, i believe,
and i pray:

Lord,
i long to be used.

## *blessings*

i am mindful:
my life is a profound blessing.
once ensnared in the shadow of bitterness and sorrow,
i overlooked the delicate traces of grace.

the path through grief, circuitous and enduring,
unwrapped the precious gifts that once lay concealed.
i've learned to mend my wounds,
without masking or forsaking my feelings,
but with compassion for myself and those i hold dear.

the irreplaceable essence of my existence,
birthed by nurturing hearts—
i'm draped in gratitude,
embracing my unique walk and irreplaceable roots;
they mold me, and for God's faithfulness,
my heart is eternally indebted.

## *the end of a chapter and the beginning of new*

if only this season's gentle sway could stretch,
its joy, an ember glowing with timeless grace,
each moment cherished, yet tales find closure,
as one chapter ends, another takes its place.

in the cradle of comfort, i sense the finale's call,
a prelude to a fresh journey, uncharted and bold;
should i probe too deeply, fear's grip may tighten,
and worldly cares, like shadows, may encroach and
    hold.

but my heart, unwavering, clings to its convictions,
in the face of skeptics and shallow doubts.
some may call it folly, others see idealistic visions,
yet their opinions hold no substance;
my life's tapestry unfolds as my beliefs weave a unique
    path.

midst the haze of doubt and my life veiled in fragility,
still i believe, and there is hope in my heart,
"in the proper time, the puzzle will complete itself."

one thing i know for sure, my friend,
this, marks the beginning of new.

***restoration, a sequel***

in the light—

darkness stay away, you don't belong here,
i'm happy where i am, don't draw near.
i may relent, perhaps a little won't hurt,
linger in gloom, bask in the dirt.

familiarity breeds comfort, i can't deny,
memories here, still make me cry.
seek the light, with all my heart,
if i let fear deceive me, i'll fall apart.

begone, darkness, you won't win this fight,
even in this place, i will remember the light.

## *epilogue: traces of the soul*

a heartfelt reflection capturing the emotional resonance of places, exploring memories intricately woven into our existence, like a treasure map of the soul.

*cologne*

in photos, memories silently speak,
wooing an inexplicable nostalgia for origin.
love's waltz, a fleeting embrace,
leaves me longing for another sweet dance.

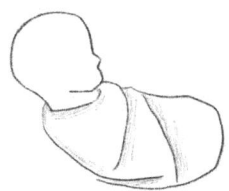

### *seoul*

a fateful pivot, i replay our farewell;
two years later—their home, now my vacation.
in bygone days, i foresaw no finale to endless summers...
yet, tearful farewells persist, growing no gentler.

## *muju*

two hearts strong, now one beats in memory,
there's no version of me without this place—how could i
    forget?
naively, we once told grandpa, 'you'll live to a hundred,'
his tears, an unforgettable response.

***orange county***

fondness of childhood, comfort,
innocence and fragility marked;
perhaps past hurts faded,
yet authenticity lives on still.

## *malibu*

lifelong friendships woven,
answered prayers.
passion's dance, perpetual growth,
a charm marked in my heart.

## *shanghai*

the sweet and the bitter,
moments cloaked in vulnerability;
young and naive, there was love,
hindsight's precious gift.

## *london*

frolicking through the streets,
redeeming memories of the past.
delight in unexpected companion,
basking in serenity.

### *los angeles*

initial fear of a big city,
turned into comfort of home.
you made me stronger,
i've grown to love you.

## *san diego*

a door unforeseen unveils,
uncertainty fills the crossroads.
faith stirring, we boldly say yes,
new beginnings in grace's sea.

## *gratitudes*

thank you, wholeheartedly, to those who walked with me through thick and thin. my beloved family, whether by the beaches of california or the warm embrace of korea, it's your steadfast love and prayers that have brought me here today. fond memories of my dear grandmother and the distant presence of yebin reside close to my heart. to my cherished friends, the ones who fill my life with joy, your thoughtful friendship is a priceless gift. to my dear friend glor, whose illustrations brought an additional resonance to these words—i'm thankful for you and the happiness in collaborating.

and to jake, my soulmate and best friend, your unwavering love has been my anchor through it all.

this collection is dedicated to lonely hearts, seeking meaning amidst the intrinsic brokenness of life. may these words offer comfort and understanding, serving as a reminder that you are never truly alone in your struggles, but that you are seen and understood. finally, i am thankful to God, the source of my strength and creativity, and for the precious gift of life.

## *about sarie*

born in cologne, germany, and raised amidst the diverse landscapes of seoul and orange county, sarie's journey now unfolds in the sun-kissed beauty of san diego, california, where she shares life with her husband—her dearest friend. creative expression has been her lifelong companion, marked by early achievements like winning a creative drawing contest in second grade and earning the best writing award in sixth grade.

with a poet's heart and a compassionate spirit, sarie delicately weaves her emotions into words, aspiring to be a source of hope for those who feel alone and disheartened. she believes, with unwavering certainty, that in every shadowed corner, light awaits—a simple truth that gently moves us forward, one step at a time.

journey with sarie: @sariewrites

www.ingramcontent.com/pod-product-compliance
Lightning Source LLC
Chambersburg PA
CBHW032041040426
42449CB00007B/967